Projects in Music
Book Three : History

Projects in Music
Book Three : History

IAN LAWRENCE

LONGMAN

LONGMAN GROUP LIMITED
London

Associated companies, branches and representatives
throughout the world

© Ian Lawrence 1967

First published 1967
Sixth impression 1975

ISBN 0 582 32553 6

Printed in Hong Kong by
Wing Tai Cheung Printing Co Ltd

Contents

Illustrations

Acknowledgements

We are grateful to the following for permission to reproduce copyright material:

Akademische Druck u. Verlagsanstalt for 'Saraband'e from *Suite XIV* by Froberger (Ed. Guido Adler); Arno Volk Verlag Hans Gerig K.G. for bars from 'Courante' by L. Couperin from *Keyboard Music of the Baroque and Rococo*, Vol. 1 (Ed. Georgii); Breitkopf & Haertel, Wiesbaden for bars from 'Pavane' by T. Morley, 'Quadran Pavane' and 'Quadran Galliard' by Bull, and 'Volta' by Byrd from *Fitzwilliam Virginal Book* (Ed. Maitland and Squire), and *Contretanze* K.510 No. 2 by Mozart; Centre National de la Recherche Scientifique for bars from 'Le Branle de Malte' by Le Roy from *Fantaisies et Danses, 1568* (Editions du C.N.R.S.— (1962); Galliard Ltd for the Mazurka by Chopin from *Augener Classics for Piano;* Editions Hinrichsen Ltd, London, the owners of Editions Peters for the 'Minuet' from *Haydn's 'A' Major Piano Sonata*, 'Bourrée' from *Second English Suite* by Bach, and 'Passepied' from *5th English Suite* by Bach; Editions de la Revue Musicale for 'Loure' from *Alceste* by Lully from the series Oeuvres Complètes de J.B. Lully 1632-1687 publiées sous la Direction de Henry Prunières; G. Ricordi & Co. (London) Ltd for the *Waltz* by Brahms, Op. 39, No. 11; G. Schirmer Inc., New York (Chappell & Co. Ltd. London) for bars from 'Gavotte' by Couperin, 'Siciliana' by Scarlatti, 'Gigue' by Rameau and 'Hornpipe' by Muffat from *Early Keyboard Music*, Vol. II; Schott, Music Publishers for an extract from *Mendelssohn's Hebrides Overture* (Eulenburg Edn.); Société de Musique d'Autrefois for bars from *Attaingnant Basse Danse* transcribed by Professor Daniel Heartz; Stainer & Bell Ltd for bars from 'Aimain' from *Suite No. 1* by M. Lock, ed. by Dart; State Publishing House of Music, Prague for the 'Polka' by Antonin Dvořák from *Dances* (Artia Edn. Prague 1961), and Ugrino Verlag for bars from 'Bergamasca' by Samuel Scheidt from *Works Book V*.

We have been unable to trace the copyright owners in 'Corrento I' by Frescobaldi and 'Canaries' by Chambonnières from *First Book of Pieces* and would welcome any information that would enable us to do so.

The cover illustration is taken from *Chorégraphie* by Feuillet, published in 1701 (British Museum).

Preface for Teachers

A strong case could be made for the total neglect of all but the immediate past as far as the teaching of musical history to the young musician is concerned. (We can be tolerably certain that the possession of the historical perspective with which we pride ourselves so much today was not thought to be among the essential qualifications of musicians until comparatively recently.)

Can we afford to spend time listening to the past before we are familiar with the present? The attitude of children is illuminating here: they have a natural delight in the present which is in many ways alien to the adult who, for various reasons, is not only more acutely aware of the past than the child, but is in a sense more dependent upon it. Without the burden of the past to carry, we might have more energy to devote to performing, writing and listening to the music of our own time.

No one, however, can grow up in this age of radio and television without being constantly exposed to the music of the past. The child is thus assaulted by a confusion of styles from an early age. Even the hymns sung each morning at school condition the ear of the young musician to the patterns of the past. Inevitably the music teacher feels an obligation to sort out this confusion into the type of comprehensible pattern which we call musical history.

But if the history of music is to be taught in schools then it has got to be something more than the type of names – dates – major-works catalogue that is so often offered under this heading. Since we cannot possibly cover the whole of musical history, the problem is, as usual, one of priorities. What are the important things about the music of the past that we wish to show to the new generation?

In the first place it is the music itself: how it employs voices or instruments and how it sets and solves its rhythmic, melodic and harmonic problems. (This should hardly need to be said, but which of us can honestly say that he has not written about a topic of musical history at some time or other for which his information is not only secondhand but based on a complete unfamiliarity with the actual music concerned?)

In the second place, the conditions (social, political and economic, etc.) which produced it. And third, the personality of the composer. Fortunately we have emerged from the dark ages of 'musical history', when the music was seen simply as the expression of the composer's feelings. But the composer's individuality is obviously absorbed in his work.

There is, of course, so much content in the music itself that many teachers may feel that there is no time to get on to the second and third stages. But it is important to remember that a piece of music written in the past is a small part of that past, and although it may be able to speak to us directly, its creation occurred in a certain place at a certain time and for particular reasons. For a deeper understanding of the music we need to be familiar with these circumstances.

Even with the greatest works of art, however, direct communication cannot be assumed. Most of us need a helping hand. Ideally this is what the music teacher should provide. But it does not always work out as simply as that. If it did, this and most other textbooks would be superfluous. The textbook, in an imperfect world, has its value.

The object of this book is to provide a framework for the study of the music of the past. The *Preliminary* sections are concerned with some of the methods of assembly and presentation that are possible in schools. Each of the five chapters which follow forms in turn an introduction to the music of the sixteenth, seventeenth, eighteenth, nineteenth and twentieth centuries, but concentrates on only one particular aspect of the history of music—*music and dancing*.

Dancing has such a fundamental association with music that no excuse is offered for selecting it in preference to other topics, e.g. Music and the church, Music and the theatre, Music and the concert hall.

Moreover these topics are already well-trodden ground, and the teacher will want to base such lessons on those works which he already has available. At the end of each chapter a summary of the forms and composers in these other fields is offered as a general guide.

The study of musical history, however, should not form an isolated aspect of our musical training. It is not enough to listen to and read about the music of the past. Performance, analysis and composition must be linked with such activity. The chapters therefore contain suggestions for linking these parts of training with the historical work.

Some teachers may find it helpful to refer to ADVANCED PROJECTS IN MUSIC if they feel that the implications of this method are made insufficiently clear at this stage.

In conclusion I would like to draw attention to three general points:
1 In order that reference is made as simple as possible, the treatment of the dances in each of the chapters is fairly uniform. It is likely, however, that in a situation in which pupils solemnly work their way through chapter after chapter the uniformity would itself undermine the concentration of the pupils. It is

important, therefore, that the teacher selects the material that he feels to be most appropriate for his class at the time, and uses the other sections for reference purposes only.

2 Some of the *Projects* will present difficulties to pupils who have no experience of the work contained in *Book One* and *Book Two*. In such cases the teacher might (*a*) adapt the work to suit the particular circumstances (*b*) introduce some of the methods found in *Books One* and *Two* where they seem appropriate.

It is not intended that *Books Three* and *Four* of this series should form part of a systematic scheme of work. Ideally they should be used concurrently and linked, where possible, to material on *Books One* and *Two*.

3 It is outside the scope of this book to offer guidance in the practical problems of actually dancing the dances mentioned here, but many teachers will recognise the value in such a course. Where it is appropriate, therefore, every effort should be made to perform the dances. If assistance is not available from dance experts, help may be obtained from some of the many books on historical dances that are available: e.g.:

DOLMETSCH, M. *Dances of England and France* 1450 – 1600 Routledge
DOLMETSCH, M. *Dances of Spain and Italy* 1400 – 1600 Routledge
SACHS, K. *World History of the Dance.* Norton
WOOD, M. *Historical Dances* (3 vols.) Imp. Soc. Teachers of Dancing

IAN LAWRENCE

MARIA GREY COLLEGE OF EDUCATION

Preliminaries

1 Looking at and listening to the past

One of the ways that we can find out about things that happened in the past is to read about them in a history book. But it is not the only way. We can discover things about the past for ourselves by visiting such places as old buildings and old towns, or by investigating museums and places where original documents are kept, and in a host of other ways.

If we want to find out about the music of earlier times we can also read about it in books. But clearly this is not enough: it is essential that we *hear* the music. Fortunately the enormous number of gramophone records that are produced today make it possible for us to listen to a great deal of the music that has been written during the last four hundred years. Moreover, historians are gradually discovering more of the music of earlier centuries and a certain amount of that belonging to the Middle Ages is already known. (In European countries, of course. Our knowledge of music outside Europe, although growing, is not yet very large.)

When we listen to the music of earlier centuries, it sounds different from the music of our own time, just as the clothes, houses, paintings, books and games of earlier centuries are different from those of today. Moreover, if we were to listen to pieces of music composed in 1550, 1650, 1750, 1850, and 1950, the first four pieces would not only sound different from the music of own time, but also very different from each other. It is very easy to think of the past being all the same, but each period of the past has its own characteristics and differs almost as much from those periods near it as those far away from it.

After a reasonable amount of study the main differences will become obvious. In fact so obvious, that it will be the similarities that demand our attention. For example, after we have decided what are the basic differences between the pieces written in 1550, 1650, 1750, 1850 and 1950, we will want to know what is similar among them, both in style and in the purpose for which they were written. To discover, in other words, whether or not one generation retains anything from an earlier one.

To recognise the differences and similarities between the music of different periods is the first problem. To understand why they occur is the second. The third problem is the observation of some sort of sequence of events in musical history, and the fourth is the important matter of presentation – that is how we make our knowledge available to other people.

Each of these problems is discussed in the following Preliminary sections:

2 Why are there changes in musical style?

3 Do the changes in musical style follow any pattern?

4 How can the information best be presented?

A person who is interested in a particular subject is usually interested in its history. The stamp collector does not only collect stamps in current usage; the railway enthusiast learns something of the older locomotives, and so on.

There are two main reasons. First, the history is fascinating in itself; second, it helps us to understand more about the present. When we are studying the history of music, however, another factor is introduced. The best pieces of music written in the past belong as much to the present as they do to the period in which they were written. In other words we can enjoy them as much for their own sake as the composer's contemporaries did – perhaps more so – that is, not as historical events, however interesting and thus enjoyable they may be, but as a vivid experience entirely related to our own lives.

This is perhaps the greatest difference between the history of an art – music, painting, sculpture, architecture, drama, poetry – and the history of events in the normal sense.

Dress

circa 1550: Edward VI painted by Holbein

right Elizabeth I painted when a Princess by Holbein

3

circa 1650: a family group painted by Cogno

circa 1750: Mr. and Mrs. Robert Andrews painted by Gainsborough

4

circa 1850: St. James's Park

London and Paris fashions, November 1850

right 1950's: W. Somerset Maugham painted by Sutherland

circa 1650: the Hall, Cotterstock, Northamptonshi

circa 1550: the President's Lodge, Queens' College, Cambridge

circa 1750: the South Facade, Kedleston Hall, Derbyshire, built by Robert Adam

circa 1850: the Red House, Bexley Heath

in the 1950's: a Housing Estate in Bracknell, Berkshire

Sea Transport

circa 1550: the *Ark Royal*

circa 1650: the *Soveraigne of the Sea*

circa 1750: the *London*

8

circa 1850: the arrival of Queen Victoria, Prince Albert and suite at Woolwich in the General Steam Navigation Ship *Trident*

A cargo boat in the 1950's

Road Transport

circa 1550: the top row shows the carriages of Elizabeth I and her maids

circa 1650: carriage outside the Sheldonian Theatre, Oxford (from an engraving by T. Hoggan)

10

circa 1750: 'The Present Age' from an engraving by L. P. Boitard

circa 1850: the *Edinburgh Express*

Road transport in the 1950's: an *Austin A-90 Atlantic Coupé*

Air transport in the 1950's:
a *Percival Prince* freight plane

Project 1
Find out which instruments were the most popular in about 1550, 1650, 1750, 1850, and 1950, and make copies of any of their pictures that you can find.

Rail Transport

circa 1850: the *Little England*

transport in 1950's: *Pacific* locomotive, *Britannia* class

2 Why are there changes in musical style?

The word 'style' is applied to music in a number of ways. Let us consider what it means in terms of a very well known work – Mendelssohn's *Hebrides Overture* (1830).

QUESTION: What is the style of the *Hebrides Overture?*

ANSWERS 1 Early *romantic* style – nineteenth century – descriptive – harmony has something in common with general European style of the period.

2 *German* romantic style – characteristics in common with other Germans of the period (Weber, Schumann, etc.) – as opposed to French style, for example.

3 *Orchestral* style – not so obvious as it sounds, since some chamber music can be said to be ' orchestral ' in style, and vice versa.

4 *Symphonic* style – in this case this is an inevitable consequence of (3), but this would not always be true, e.g. Bach Orchestral Suite.

5 *Early Mendelssohn* style – it shares features of harmony, melody, structure, etc., which are common to all Mendelssohn's work of that period.

6 Vigorous, dramatic, descriptive of the sea, etc. – i.e. your personal feeling about the work as a separate, individual work of art.

If there are so many answers to this question, then there will probably be several answers to the question 'Why are there changes in musical style?"
Because:

1 The music of every generation reflects, to a certain extent, the particular interests and hopes of that generation since it is one of the means of communication which people use.

2 The music of a particular country or region may reflect the changing circumstances of that place.

3 Music written for instruments is influenced by changes in the materials used and the methods employed by the craftsmen.

4 Music that is written for such well defined occasions as church services, for example, must suit the varying circumstances that the clergy and congregation impose.

5 Every composer will inevitably acquire individual characteristics of style.

6 Music is constantly influenced by changing social political and economic factors.

Only a few of the explanations have been set out here. You will no doubt be able to suggest some more.

In addition to these particular points there can be recognised a factor which we can call 'taste' or 'fashion.' People often talk about 'good taste' and 'bad taste', and 'in fashion' and 'out of fashion'.

It is very difficult to say exactly what is meant by such expressions, or how changes in taste or fashion occur. Nevertheless it is important to acknowledge their existence, for another answer to our question is 'because fashions change.' The answer does not get us very far, but it suggests the influence of purely social factors which we cannot ignore.

Project 2
Study another piece of music with which you are familiar, and find out how many answers you can provide to the question: 'What is the style of this piece of music?'

3 Do the changes in musical style follow any pattern?
The answer to this question is both 'yes' and 'no'. Yes, it is possible to see certain things recurring from time to time in musical history. For example in about the years 1300, 1600, and 1900, the idea that 'new' means of musical expression were widespread is suggested by the titles applied to the music of those times: *Ars Nova, Nuove Musiche,* and The New Music.

On the other hand, most attempts to prove that musical history, or indeed history in general, follows any clearly defined order usually ends in the facts being 'arranged' to fit the theories, rather than reverse. Here are a few of the obviously *wrong* ideas about musical history:
1 That musical history is simply the history of the 'great composers'.
2 That musical history is connected with Darwin's 'evolutionary' theory. (CHARLES DARWIN *The Origin of Species,* 1859).
3 That there exist well defined 'periods' of history containing starting and finishing points with 'experimental' works at the beginning and 'mature' works at the end.
4 That the path followed by the history of music is identical to that followed by the other arts.
5 That musical history is a type of pendulum swinging between various opposites: e.g. counterpoint and harmony, nationalism and internationalism, vocal and instrumental styles, etc.

Project 3

Discuss as many of the above ideas as you can. If you disagree with any of the points, don't be afraid to say so – but you must back up your opinions with examples.

4 How can the information best be presented?

There are a number of ways in which you can present the information that you have collected. Briefly, they can be in the form of:

1 Notes.
2 Essays.
3 Displays or exhibitions.
4 Lectures with musical illustrations.
5 Concerts with programme notes.

Which you choose will depend upon the purpose for which the information is collected. Notes should be clear and concise and properly organised under main headings. Their purpose is to summarise the important points of any topic, and to provide you with an immediate guide to the principal developments.

Essays have an altogether different function. In addition to presenting the facts in a style which is pleasant to read, they are usually concerned with discussing the significance of such information. It is very important that musical examples should be quoted where they can illuminate a point that you are trying to make.

Displays and exhibitions can be very useful in presenting historical material. Examples of instruments, concert halls, theatres, churches, publications, original notation, scores or other interesting material which is related to a topic that you are studying, can often help to clear up all sorts of difficulties. But normally a musical subject demands that the music be heard, which in the normal way displays do not provide.

Short lectures or talks with the use of live or recorded examples therefore provide an excellent companion to such exhibitions. Actual concerts with some sort of spoken or written commentary is perhaps the best conclusion to an extended piece of research into a particular aspect of musical history. In such cases we cannot be in danger of talking about music that we have never heard!

Project 4

Organise an exhibition of musical instruments. Employ competent demonstrators for each instrument. Try to find pictures of instruments that are the ancestors of the ones on display. Draw diagrams to show how the instruments work, for example:

The action of keyboard instruments.

The valve systems of brass instruments.

The key systems of woodwind instruments.

Lady playing a lute,
from an engraving by Tobias Stimmer

Music and Dancing

Today dancing is just another form of entertainment. It has not always been so. Until perhaps as late the fifteenth century in Western Europe, and until much more recent time in other parts of the world, dancing had very strong connections with both religious rituals and magical rites.

It is, however, its influence on the music of the last five hundred years that chiefly interests us here. For during this period dancing has not only been of the most important forms of entertainment in Europe, but it has also influenced the development of instrumental music to a remarkable extent.

Dance music has these obvious features: the need for a clear pulse, interesting rhythmic patterns, and easily repeatable phrases. It is the need for strong rhythmic patterns and the necessity of varying the continually repeated phrases that has constantly fascinated the composer. And so in addition to writing music merely for dancing as such, he has written an enormous quantity of music based on dance forms, but intended chiefly for people to play for their entertainment, or simply to listen to.

Virginals

Harpsichord

Such *players'* or *listeners'* dances have been written from the sixteenth century until our own times. In the sixteenth century the LUTE and the VIRGINALS were the most popular choice of instrument for such pieces. In the seventeenth century the HARPSICHORD and the SMALL ORCHESTRA take over, and continue to dominate the scene well into the eighteenth century. Towards the end of this period the harpsichord is replaced by the PIANO as the principal keyboard instrument, but the great demand for dance movements goes on unchanged. With the growth in size of the orchestra in the nineteenth century, the dance remains a popular form of composition. In the twentieth century dances have been written not only for the FULL ORCHESTRA but for an ever increasing range of soloists and ensembles. The re-awakening of interest in the older forms of composition, particularly of the sixteenth and seventeenth centuries has in some cases been accompanied by the revived use of some of the older instruments, especially the recorder and the harpsichord.

It has been common practice for composers to join a number of dances together as a set of pieces. The name usually given to such a set is the SUITE, but the French have used the word ORDRE, the Germans PARTITA, and the Italians SONATA DA CAMERA (room, chamber) to describe the same thing.

The suite begins, perhaps, with the pairing of dances in the sixteenth century with the BASSE DANCE and an 'afterdance', e.g. SALTARELLO. These were succeeded by the PAVANE and GALLIARD or the PASSAMEZZO and SALTARELLO. The seventeenth century saw the ALLEMANDE and the COURANTE forming such a pair, but most suites by now contained other dances such as the SARABANDE and GIGUE.

The distinguished German composer FROBERGER (1617–1667) used the four dances as the movements of many of his suites (which usually concluded with the sarabande). PURCELL (1659–1695) also uses them, but does not often include the gigue (jig) in his suites (lessons), which is surprising, for the gigue is often thought to be the only English contribution to the suite. The great Italian composer CORELLI (1653–1713) wrote many suites (under the title *sonata da camera*) and helped to establish the practice of preceding the actual dances with an introductory movement called a PRELUDE.

In France COUPERIN (1668–1733) and RAMEAU (1683–1764) published a vast quantity of 'ordres', but did not restrict themselves to any particular pattern of dances nor simply to the dance names, preferring to group large sets of pieces, each with descriptive titles such as 'Les Papillons' (butterflies), 'Les Petits Moulins à Vent' (windmills), or 'Les Moissonneurs' (reapers). The suites of HANDEL (1685–1759) were mostly written for his pupils, and possibly for that reason are less exciting than those of BACH (1685–1750).

In addition to the prelude, allemande, courante and gigue (which was now generally accepted as the most suitable closing movement), Bach usually included a number of other dances in his suites. These 'extra' dances (in German: GALANTERIEN, in Italian: INTERMEZZI) would be found between the sarabande and the gigue, and would include the GAVOTTE, BOURRÉE, MINUET, PASSEPIED, POLONAISE, ANGLAISE and the LOURE, but only one or two of these would be selected for each suite. It is important to notice that at this time the 'Galanterien' were the only members of the suite that really still sounded like the original simple peasant dances. The allemandes, courantes, sarabandes and

20

gigues, although still recognisable as dances, were now written in such a complex style that it was generally impossible to dance to them.

By the second half of the eighteenth century the suite had been superseded by the sonata and the symphony. Only the minuet survived the transplantation, although many symphonic finales retain a certain similarity with the gigue.

Although after 1750 the dance suite gradually disappears, composers nevertheless continued to base many of their pieces on dance forms. Many new dances were introduced, including the ÉCOSSAISE, MAZURKA, POLKA, WALTZ and a later style of the POLONAISE. The waltz in particular attracted considerable interest from nearly all the leading nineteenth century composers.

In the twentieth century, the enthusiasm shown by Western European composers for the dance forms of countries outside their own area greatly increased, and in particular the dances of South America and the United States became very popular. Moreover the rise in the nineteenth century of musical nationalism (in the countries surrounding the central core of France, Germany and Italy) meant that the dances of Russia, Czechoslovakia, Hungary, Greece, Spain and others were brought into the reach of European composers in general.

In the chapters which follow the most important dances have been loosely grouped under the centuries in which they had the most influence on instrumental forms (i.e. not necessarily in the centuries in which they were most popular actually as dances). Where it is appropriate, a list of *modern* works which use the older dances is included.

The Sixteenth Century

It was not until the late fifteenth century that professional dance teachers appeared in Europe, and not until the early sixteenth century that music printing was established. With these two facts in mind, therefore, we would not expect to find very much in the way of *listeners'* dance music until the end of the century.

Nevertheless, some important collections of dances have survived, including volumes from the following printers:

PETRUCCI in Venice: lute books from 1507, including the pavane, saltarello, and gagliarda.

ATTAIGNANT in Paris: lute books from 1529 with the basse dance, branle, pavane and galliard.

LE ROY in Paris: lute books from 1539 (he was probably the most successful lutanist of the period).

SUSATO in Antwerp: lute books from 1551 (again basse dance, pavanes and galliards).

The printer ANTICO, in Rome, published music from as early as 1514, but mostly confined himself to vocal music. These four cities – Venice, Paris, Antwerp and Rome – represent the four main centres of European music during the major part of the sixteenth century. Spanish influence was of course very important, but most Spanish music found an outlet in Antwerp or Rome.

It was not until the close of the sixteenth century that English music printing established itself in London with the guidance of TALLIS (*c.* 1505–1585), BYRD (1543–1623) and MORLEY (1557–1603), three of the most important figures in English music of that period. But English interest in continental dance forms dates from much earlier in the century. In 1521, a certain Robert Copelande published a little English–French vocabulary which ended with an outline of 'the maner of dauncying of bace daunces after the style of France and other places'.

Although Italy, Spain and France were the leading countries for dancing in the century, England under Elizabeth (1558–1603) made great progress. At the Court, dancing became probably the most important single accomplishment for the courtier. The Spanish pavane and the French galliard were the most popular dances, and the standards of the court were set by the Queen herself, who was said to dance as many as four or five galliards *before breakfast*.

Elizabeth I, 1533–1603

The pavane lost its leading place in court dancing to the Italian passamezzo (passy-measures in English) during the second half of the century, but nevertheless it remained a very important form in instrumental music. The English virginals composers in particular used it a lot, and the number of pavanes that have survived is far greater than galliards, despite the fact that the galliard continued to be danced long after the pavane had been superceded. As with other dances, the pavane was often used as the subject of a series of variations in which the decoration of the main theme gradually became more elaborate.

Some of our information about sixteenth century dances comes from books published at the end of the century. Of these, the most important are:

SIR JOHN DAVIES *Orchestra – a poem on the antiquity and excellency of Dancing* (1596)

THOMAS MORLEY *Plain and Easy Introduction to Practical Music* (1597)

FABRITIO CAROSO *Il Ballarino* (1581) Italian

THOINOT ARBEAU *Orchésographie* (1588) French

Arbeau's book is probably the most important and has been translated into modern English. Thoinot Arbeau was the pen-name of a French priest whose

Pied ioinct oblique droict.

Pied ioinct oblique gaulche.

Line drawings from *Orchésographie* by Arbeau, published in 1588

real name was Jehan Tabourot. The title of his book, *Orchésographie*, means 'the study of dancing'.

It consists of a long conversation between Arbeau and his pupil Capriol (*It capriolare* = to caper or dance) in which all the main French dances of the century are discussed:

Basse dance		25
Pavane		28
Galliard	refer to page	31
Volta		33
Branles		33

Courante		44
Allemande	refer to page	43
Gavotte		79

Bouffons (sword dances,etc)
Morisque (Morris Dance)

The first five of these dances, together with the Italian passamèzzo and saltarello, were often written as instrumental pieces by many of the leading European composers. The courante, allemande and gavotte had to wait until later times to establish themselves as instrumental forms.

24

Pied croiſé droiƈt.   Pied croiſé gaulche.

Capriol.

Voila deſia de pluſieurs ſortes de geſtes & mouuements.

Arbeau.

Il vous tarde(à ce que ie peulx cognoiſtre) que vous com-
mēciez a faire les cinq pas,mais il ny a remede, il fault que vous

Line drawings from *Orchésographie* by Arbeau, published in 1588

When we are thinking about these dances it is important to remember that the court dress would naturally restrict the dancers' movements. Refer, if you can, to pictures of the costumes of the centuɪy, and compare them with those of other periods. Nor should we forget that each dance had its individual steps, and that familiarity with the main steps and many minor variations, was expected of the ordinary dancer, and not simply from a few professionals.

Basse Dance *Fr* Bassadanza *It* Baxa Danza *Sp*
This slow and stately dance was popular in the first half of the century and had been known as far back as the fourteenth. As far as we can discover it consisted of simple and double gliding steps, accompanied by gracious bows and a gentle swaying movement. The music often consisted of an improvised tune over a repeated bass part. This may explain the origin of the name, but it might also have come from 'bas' meaning 'low' (in contrast to the *danse haute* (high) or *sautée* (jumped), i.e. the saltarello with which it was often paired.) The basse dance was usually in duple time (i.e. $\mathbb{C}$ ($\frac{2}{2}$) or $\frac{6}{4}$ $\downarrow$. $\downarrow$.).

Attaignant published eighteen for lute in 1529, two for keyboard in 1530, and nine for instrumental ensemble in 1530.

Here is a transcription of one of the lute dances:

ANALYSIS

Melody	Horizontal interval	Movement mostly by step
	Phrase	Two bars long
Harmony	Vertical interval	Lute spacing, no discords
	Counterpoint	Simple imitation in two parts
Rhythm	Rhythmic pattern	
	Pace	Moderately slow
Form	Repetition	A B A
	Contrast	Three-part chords and hint of key change

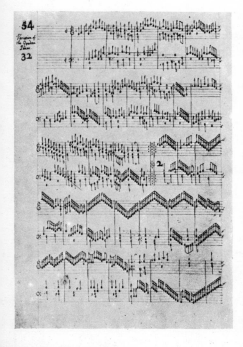

Variation of the *Quadran Pavan*,
page 54 of the Fitzwilliam Virginal Book

Modern version:

WARLOCK *Capriol Suite*, Basse Dance

Project 5

Write or improvise a short piece (about twelve bars) based on the basse dance rhythm. Remember that the most important point is the two strong beats to the bar. Thus, $\frac{2}{2}$, $\frac{2}{4}$, $\frac{6}{4}$, or $\frac{6}{8}$ are the most suitable time signatures. Try to capture the stately atmosphere of the dance.

The basse dance was nearly always followed by a quicker dance with *three* beats to the bar. It appears under a great many different titles in both the fifteenth and sixteenth centuries. Perhaps the easiest name to remember it by is the AFTERDANCE. In Italy it was often called the SALTARELLO (*It* saltare =to jump). Generally it would contain the same melodic ideas as the basse dance, but changed from a two beat version into one with three beats. This practice became very popular in many forms of instrumental composition, including those not actually based on dance rhythms, such as *canzonas*, *intradas*, and *ricercars*.

(See also the SALTARELLO in the NINETEENTH CENTURY, p. 108.)

Pavane (*Sp* pavo=peacock)

The pavane is probably the most famous sixteenth-century dance. It was a slow, dignified dance in $\frac{2}{2}$ time, with much simpler patterns of steps than the basse dance which it generally replaced. The sight of the long trailing dresses of the ladies of the court as they processed down the ballroom with their partners no doubt suggested the strutting movements of the peacock, and thus provided a name for the dance.

It was particulary popular in England, and all the composers of keyboard music included the pavane in their sets of pieces. The best examples are perhaps those of BYRD, BULL, GIBBONS, MORLEY and DOWLAND. Here is an example:

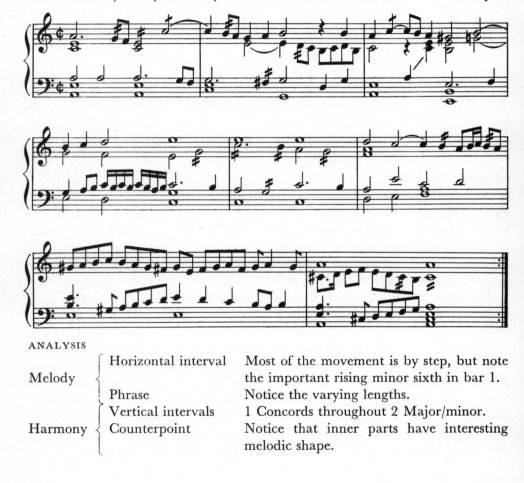

ANALYSIS

Melody	Horizontal interval	Most of the movement is by step, but note the important rising minor sixth in bar 1.
	Phrase	Notice the varying lengths.
Harmony	Vertical intervals	1 Concords throughout 2 Major/minor.
	Counterpoint	Notice that inner parts have interesting melodic shape.

28

Rhythm	Rhythmic pattern	Complex patterns over strong two beat pattern.
	Pace	Slow, but must move *forwards*.
Form	Repetition / Contrast	(Achieved in variations which follow.)

This pavane is by Morley: it is followed by a series of quite long variations, which develop the ideas of these opening eight bars. The tune, however, is not Morley's, but Dowland's. Dowland was principally a composer for the lute, and he wrote this beautiful *Lachrymae Pavane* for that instrument. However, it so fascinated the other composers of the time that many of them made their own settings of the tune for virginals.

This piece can be found in a collection of music for the virginals called the FITZWILLIAM VIRGINAL BOOK. This is a wonderful collection of nearly three hundred compositions which were written down by an Elizabethan enthusiast.

The original manuscript has been preserved in the Fitzwilliam Museum in Cambridge. It provides us with a large quantity of music which we would otherwise not have known, for very little keyboard music was actually printed at the time. Nearly all the leading Elizabethan instrumental composers are represented, including:

John Bull	1562–1628	Thomas Morley	1557–1603
William Byrd	1543–1623	Peter Philips	? –1630
Giles Farnaby	1565–1640	Thomas Tomkins	1572–1657
Orlando Gibbons	1583–1625		

Project 6

Find out as much as you can about the music written by these composers, and write a short biography of at least one of them.

In Italy the pavane had generally been replaced by the PASSAMEZZO by about 1550. There are at least three possible explanations of this term:
1 Passo (step) mezzo (half), i.e. the pavane in half steps (thus twice as quick?).
2 Passo e mezzo, i.e. step *and* a half – a new version of the pavane step?
3 Bassa mezzo, the middle or halfway section of the basse dance.
If its origin was in fact from the basse dance, then it shares with that dance the

idea of the repeated bass line or chord sequence. Two versions of the passa-mezzo series of chords were known, one called the passamezzo ANTICO (based on the minor key) and the passamezzo MODERNO (based on the major key). The latter was often called the QUADRO (see page 32 for *Quadran Pavane* and *Galliard* by Bull). It is possible that in England at least, PASSAMEZZO indi-cated a style rather than a dance as such: for in the Fitzwilliam Virginal Book we find works by both Byrd and Philips called *Passamezzo Pavana* and *Galliarda Passamezzo*. Clearly if *passamezzo* were being used in the strict sense (i.e. a $\frac{2}{2}$ dance it could not be applied to the galliard (a $\frac{3}{4}$ dance). It was popular in England for some time where it was generally called the PASSY-MEASURES, or simply the MEASURES.

The following more recent versions of the pavane provide interesting listening:
BRITTEN Pavane from *Five Courtly Dances from Gloriana*
FAURÉ Pavane in F sharp minor
RAVEL Pavane pour une enfante défunte
SAINT-SAËNS Pavane from the ballet *Etienne Marcel*
TCHAIKOVSKY Pavane from *The Sleeping Beauty*
VAUGHAN WILLIAMS Pavane of the Heavenly Host from the ballet *Job*
WARLOCK Pavane from the *Capriol Suite*

Project 7
Write or improvise a pavane of about eight bars for one or more instruments.

Project 8
Here is the traditional ground-bass melody for the passamezzo moderno.

With the instruments that you have available, add melodic parts above this bass.

FIRST STAGE: use only the notes of the common chord, e.g.

30

SECOND STAGE: add passing notes, e.g.

THIRD STAGE: add *accented* passing notes, e.g.

Galliard *Fr* (gaillard=gay) Galliarda *It*

Although the galliard probably originated in Italy, it is generally thought of as a French dance. It was very popular in France in the early part of the century, and spread to England in the latter part, where it was sometimes called the 'sink-a-pace' (cinque pace), referring to the five main steps of the dance.

In Elizabethan England every gentleman was expected to be able to dance the galliard, and the Queen herself set very high standards of attainment. Shakespeare refers to the dance several times, as, for example, in *Twelfth Night* (Act 1, Sc. 3):

Sir Toby Belch What is thy excellence in a galliard, knight?

Sir Andrew Aguecheek Faith, I can cut a caper.

It is very likely that the galliard was regarded as something more than just a dance: almost a form of athletic training!

The dance was in $\frac{3}{4}$ time as a rule, and was somewhat quicker than the pavane, with which it was normally linked. (The music was not so much quicker than the pavane, but the more vigorous steps of the galliard made it seem so.) It was quite common to find the two dances sharing the same melodic ideas, i.e. one a $\frac{2}{2}$ version, the other a $\frac{3}{4}$.

31

Here are the openings of two such dances. They are the *Quadran Pavane and Galliard* by Bull (from the Fitzwilliam Virginal Book).

BULL *The Quadran Pavane*

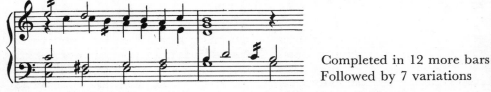

Completed in 12 more bars
Followed by 7 variations

BULL *The Quadran Galliard*

Completed in 11 more bars
Followed by 11 variations

Project 9

Analyse these two extracts, and compare the ways that the same melodic ideas are used in both pieces.

Volta *It* (=turn) Lavolta *Eng*

This was one of the first dances in which the dancers actually held each other. There was a very good reason for such a development, for it contained many swift turns and leaps, and the lady was frequently lifted high into the air. The tempo was slightly faster than the galliard (although time had to be allowed for the jumping and lifting, so it could not have been too fast), and the $\frac{6}{8}$ rhythm was common.

Although it is a less famous dance than the galliard, for example, it was clearly well known in England in Shakespeare's time, as the following reference suggests:

Duke of Bourbon They bid us to the English dancing schools. And teach *lavoltas* high and swift corantos. (*Henry V*, Act 3, Sc 5)

In fact it attracted considerable attention for quite a long time, being popular in court circles from the time of its introduction to Paris in about 1560 until well into the seventeenth century.

Here is an example by BYRD:

Project 10

Make an analysis of this short extract.

Branle (*Fr* branler=to swing or to sway)

Brando *It* Brangill or Brantle or Bransle or Brawl *Eng*

The branle was a general name for a type of dance involving *sideways* steps by rows of dancers holding hands to form a chain or circle. There were many variations of this pattern, and in fact Arbeau (see page 23) lists as many as twenty-three types of branles. Some of these later became known by individual titles, such as the Passepied (see page 75) which was the branle of the Brittany area. The *branle double*, the *branle simple* and most of the others were danced to the same rhythms as the pavane, i.e. $\frac{2}{2}$ or $\frac{4}{4}$. But at least two, the *branle gay* and the *branle de Poitou*, were in $\frac{3}{4}$ time.

The English word brawl gives in its modern sense the wrong idea of the dance, for far from being a rough or violent dance, it was generally quite smooth and gentle. An example of confusion between the two meanings occurs in another Shakespeare play *Love's Labour Lost* (Act 3, Sc 1):

Moth Master will you win your love with a French brawl?

Armado How meanest thou? brawling in French?

Moth No, my complete master; but to jig off a tune at the tongue's end, canary
to it with your feet

The following extract is the opening of a branle by the French lutanist-composer
LE ROY, published in 1568:

Review of the sixteenth century

Music in the Church	Italy	France	Germany Austria	England	Others
Forms: Vocal					*Flemish*
Mass	Ferabosco	Bourgeois	Praetorius	Byrd	Arcadelt
Service	Festa	Goudimel	Gallus	Morley	Clemens-
Motet	Gabrieli A.	Titelouze	Hassler	Tallis	non-papa
Anthem	Gabrieli G.			Taverner	Gombert
Chorale	Merulo			Tye	Josquin
	Monte			Gibbons	Lassus
	Palestrina				Sweelinck
	Rore				Willaert
Forms: Instrumental					*Spain*
Ricercar					Morales
In Nomine					Victoria
Fantasia					

Music in the Home or Court (other than dance music)	Italy	France	Germany Austria	England	Others
Forms: Vocal					
Madrigal	Ferabosco	Jannequin	Praetorius	Byrd	*Flemish*
Canzonet	Festa	Le Roy	Gallus	Bull	
Chanson	Gabrieli A.	Passereau	Hassler	Campion	Gombert
Frottola	Gabrieli G.	Costeley		Dowland	Josquin
Song (with	Merulo	Claudin		Farnaby	Lassus
lute etc.)	Monte	Attaignant		Weelkes	Willaert
	Palestrina			Wilbye	
Forms: Instrumental	Rore			Gibbons	*Spain*
				Morley	Cabezon
Fancy (Fantasia)					
Canzona					
Intrada					
Ricercar					

Revision Questions

1 Who wrote
   (a) *Plain and Easy Introduction . . .?*
   (b) *Orchésographie?*
   (c) *Lachrymae Pavane?*
   (d) *The Capriol Suite?*

2 What is
   (a) The Fitzwilliam Virginal Book?
   (b) the passy-measures?
   (c) the sink-a-pace?
   (d) the brawl?

3 Why is the
   (a) passamezzo possibly connected with the basse dance?
   (b) branle different from all the other sixteenth century dances?
   (c) pavane the most famous sixteenth century dance?
   (d) lute so important?

4 What are the most important characteristics of the
   (a) pavane?
   (b) galliard?
   (c) basse dance?
   (d) volta?

5 Which were the most important countries, musically speaking, in the sixteenth century?

Galileo Galilei, 1564–1642

The Seventeenth Century

The seventeenth century saw many changes in Europe. Spanish power gradually declined, and the Thirty Year War left Germany economically ruined. The Civil War severely limited England's power, while France established a strong central government for the first time. Scientific discoveries by Galileo, Boyle, Newton and Harvey, were accompanied by new ways of thinking exemplified by the philosophers Descartes, Spinoza and Locke.

It was also a century of change as far as music was concerned. Operas, oratorios, concertos and sonatas began to dominate the musical scene, and the Italian composers continued to be the most influential in Europe. The practice of writing variations on a dance tune which was so popular with the English virginalists, soon became very common in Italy. But it was not only keyboard instruments that attracted such pieces, but every possible combination of strings (including the new, powerful violin family, as well as viols, lutes and guitars), and wind (including flutes, recorders, bassoons and cornetts). The pairing of movements continued to be popular in the early part of the century, the ALLEMANDE and CORRENTO now replacing the older couplings. Dance rhythms also continued to be found in other instrumental forms such as the

37

Louis XIV, 1638–1715

RICERCAR (*It* ricercare=to search), CANZONA (*It*=song, but applied to instruments) and *intrada* (*It*=entrance) as well as in the new *Sonatas* for two, three or four instruments. In the early years MONTEVERDI (1567–1643) and FRESCO-BALDI (1583–1643) set the pace. In the later years VITALI (1644–1692) and CORELLI (1653–1713) were the leaders.

Italy's great musical rival at this time was France. After the establishment of a central government in the early part of the century, France settled down to a period of stablity under Louis XIV, 'le Roi Soleil' (1643–1715). His court at Versailles was the most brilliant and cultured in Europe, and dancing was perhaps even more important there than it had been in England under Elizabeth. The French King not only established a large court orchestra ('Les Vingt-quatre violins du Roy') plus the 'Chambre du Roy', (a group of instrumentalists which included lutes, guitars, flutes, oboes and some brass), but also founded the ROYAL ACADEMY OF DANCING in Paris in 1661. Dancing in the French court was often combined with a drama to produce the first developments of the ballet, and called the BALLET DE COUR (court ballet). The combination of dancing (especially when it was directed by the King's dancing master, Beauchamps), music (especially that by Lully(1632–1687)) and drama (especially that of Molière), brought great fame to Louis XIV's court.

Jean Baptiste Lully, 1632–1687

Many of the court dances had originated as peasant dances from various parts of France. The map on page 43 shows the source of a number of them. The *ballet de cour* used many of these simple dances in the very elaborate surroundings of Versailles. In addition, many of the dances became well known in other parts of Europe through their appearances in the suite.

The suite, or ORDRE, became increasingly established during the seventeenth century as a popular form of instrumental music. The French composers did not, however, restrict themselves to any set order of dances, but simply strung together a number of movements (often with variations). In the early part of the century the lute was regarded as the most important instrument by the aristocracy, and the French lutanist composers wrote a considerable number of dances for them. Chief among this group was GAULTIER (1603–1672), whose dance pieces mostly had descriptive titles in the English virginalist tradition. The main dances used were the allemande, courante and sarabande, but the gigue, pavane, chaconne and canarie were often included.

The term CLAVECIN was generally used for the French keyboard instruments, and might include the clavichord, spinet or harpsichord. The first important clavecin composer was CHAMBONNIÈRES (1602–1672), whose style was very similar to Gaultier's. D'ANGLEBERT (1635–1691) and LOUIS COUPERIN (1626–1661) were two other important composers in this field.

D

In England the Elizabethan passion for dancing underwent some changes. As in France, straightforward court dancing had to compete with the MASQUE, which was similar in some ways to the French ballet de cour, but tended to place more emphasis on the purely dramatic aspects. This was partly determined by the great dramatist Ben Jonson, whose influence tilted the balance of music and drama heavily in favour of the drama.

Under Charles I (1625–1649) the court became very strongly influenced by French culture (Charles married Henrietta Maria, sister of Louis XIII) and many of the French dances reached England during this time. In addition, however, the interest in English COUNTRY DANCES became very widespread.

It is sometimes thought that the Commonwealth and Protectorate (1649–1659) did tremendous harm to music. While it is true that it interrupted the natural development of music in the church, court and theatre, it is by no means correct to assume that its influence was bad in every direction. Instrumental music continued to flourish and the general enthusiasm for dancing and dance music, if anything increased. In 1651 the first edition of John Playford's *The English Dancing Master* was published.

This was a set of 'Plaine and easie Rules for the Dancing of Country Dances, with the Tune to each Dance', and it was such a success that new editions continued to appear frequently well into the eighteenth century. Country dancing had in fact been popular in the Elizabethan court, but in the seventeenth century they achieved their greatest fame. In the Restoration period the link between the dancing at court and dancing by country people was very strong. These dances were usually performed to arrangements of popular songs of the day, and do not seem to have established any strong individual characteristics. Consequently they did not attract the attention of composers in the way that the pavane had so convincingly done. The English suite, therefore, tended to imitate its continental rivals, and be chiefly based on the almand, corant, and saraband, as they were then called. Purcell (1659–1695) dominated the English scene during the latter part of the century, and contributed a set of eight 'lessons', as his suites were called. The most important of Purcell's predecessors were SIMPSON (d. 1669), JENKINS (1592–1678) and LOCKE (1630–1677).

In Germany the influence of English composers was very strong in the early part of the century, and the pavans and galliard for a long time rivalled the allemande and courante. Dances for various groups of string and wind instruments were written by MELCHIOR FRANK (d. 1639), SCHEIDT (d. 1654), SCHEIN

All in a Garden green   *Longwayes for fix*

Lead up all a D. forwards and back, Set and turne S. :. That again :.

Firft man fhake his owne Wo. by the hand, then the 2 then the 3 by one hand, then by the other, kiffe her twice and turne her :. Shake her by the hand, then the 2. then your owne by one hand, then by the other ; kiffe her twice and turn her :.

Sides all, fet and turne S. :. That again :.   This as before, the We, doing it :.

Armes all, fet and turne S :. That againe :.   This as before, the man doing it :.

Sedanny, or Dargafon   *For as many as will ftanding thus*

Firft man and Wo. fides once fet and turne S. :. Paffe forward each to the next fides, fet and turne S. :. As much to the next :. and fo forward and back till you come to your places where you began.

Armes all as you fided, till you come to your owne places.

The fingle Hey all handing as you paffe till you come to your places.

A page from *The English Dancing Master* by John Playford, 1651

41

Henry Purcell, 1658–1695 from a drawing by Godfrey Kneller

(d. 1630) and SCHEIDEMAN (d, 1663). (N.B. The fourth, and most important 'S' in German seventeenth-century music – SCHÜTZ (1585–1672) – is missing from the list because he did not contribute to instrumental dance music.)

In the middle of the century FROBERGER (1617–1667), a pupil of the great Frescobaldi, was the most influential keyboard composer. He visited North Germany, Italy, France and England from his home in Vienna, where he was court organist, and his suites reflect this international background. Froberger was followed by a number of German composers who are often thought of as simply the ' forerunners ' of Bach. The pre-eminence of Bach should not, however, blind us to the qualities of the many talented composers who immediately preceded him. In particular BUXTEHUDE (1637–1707) and PACHELBEL (1653–1706) wrote a number of entertaining suites.

The A – C – S – gigue (optional) pattern established by Froberger was the usual formula,* varied occasionally with other dances, particularly French ones.

* i.e. allemande, courante, sarabande (See also page 69).

Map showing the origin of some French dances
of the seventeenth and eighteenth centuries

Allemande *Fr* (=German dance) Alman, almain *Eng*
Although the allemande had been known from about 1550, it did not really
establish itself until the beginning of the seventeenth century, when it began to
replace the pavane and the passemezzo as the standard 2 or 4 beat slow dance.
It remained an important member of the suite long after the dance had disappeared from the ballrooms, and since it came always at the beginning of the
suite, it gradually took on the character of a prelude rather than just a dance.
The following rhythm became recognisable in many allemandes of a later period:

But in the seventeenth century more complex rhythms were often used. Here is
an example by the English composer LOCKE who was one of the numerous
instrumental composers working during the Commonwealth period.

43

LOCKE *Suite* 1: *Almain*

(First section of binary movement)

Project 11
Find out what you can about the Commonwealth period, and in particular the social customs and entertainments of the time.

Project 12
Compare this seventeenth-century allemande with an eighteenth-century example, e.g. by Bach, Handel, Teleman or Fischer.

Courante *Fr* (courir = to run) Corrento *It* Corant *Eng*
This dance was the three beat coupling with the allemande. It was very popular in France and Italy in particular, but the versions found in these two countries were often so different that we usually make it clear which we mean by using two distinct words: *courante* for the French style, and *corrento* for the Italian type.

The courante was especially popular in the court of Louis XIV and usually incorporated some of the following features:
1 $\frac{3}{2}$, mostly dotted rhythms.
2 Phrases starting on the last quaver of the bar.
3 $\frac{6}{4}$ rhythm (**123 4**56) in the closing bars.
4 Polyphonic texture in the keyboard style.

The corrento contrasted with it in the following ways:

44

1 $\frac{3}{2}$ or $\frac{3}{4}$, generally of smooth running passages.

2 More rapid tempo.

3 No complicated changes of rhythms.

Both forms remained in constant use well into the eighteenth century, and German composers, including Bach, used both forms.

Here is an example of a COURANTE:

(First half of binary piece.)

Here is an example of a CORRENTO:

(Followed by sixteen bars modulating through A minor, C major, F major, and returning to D minor.)

Girolamo Frescobaldi, 1583–1643

The Courante is by LOUIS COUPERIN (1626–1661). He was the uncle of the more famous Francois Couperin (called 'Le Grand') and a pupil of Chambonnières. He was an organist and clavecinist at the Court, and might have been as well known as his nephew if he had not died at the age of thirty-five. The Corrento is by FRESCOBALDI (1583–1643), who was for some time the chief organist of the great church of St Peter's in Rome. He is best known as a composer of organ music, but he also left a large collection of suites for the harpsichord.

Project 13
Make a very careful analysis of the rhythmic patterns of both these dances, and compare the differences.

Sarabande *Fr Ger Eng* Sarabanda *Sp It*
This dance was probably named after an instrument, the *zarabanda*, a type of flute found in Central America. It is very likely that the dance was first seen danced to this instrument, and was named after it.

The sarabande is an example of the many dances that started life fairly quick in style and gradually slowed down. By the eighteenth century it was regarded by composers as the most stately and sombre dance in the suite. Yet when it was first introduced to Europe at the end of the sixteenth century it was so vigorous and extravagant that it was officially banned by Philip II and very serious punishments were authorised against those who persisted in dancing it.

Nevertheless, the sarabande survived, and became a permanent member of the suite throughout the seventeenth and eighteenth centuries. The time signature is usually $\frac{3}{4}$, or $\frac{3}{2}$, and there is often a feeling of a strong accent on the second beat. The more dramatic sarabandes of the later years of the century are often characterised by dotted rhythms and florid decoration.

This Sarabande is part of the suite for harpsichord in G minor by the German composer FROBERGER (1617–1667). Most of his life was spent in Vienna where he was famous as the court organist. He travelled widely, however, and while he was in Rome he studied with the great Italian organist and composer Frescobaldi.

Notice that the G minor key signature has no E flat. Generally speaking, B flat was the only key signature (other than *no* sharps or flats) that was used at the time.

Project 14

Make an analysis of this sarabande on the lines of those made for earlier pieces.

Project 15

With the instruments that you have available, improvise a sarabande melody over this bass:

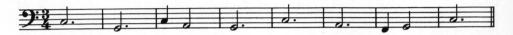

Write out your best improvisations.

Rigaudon *Fr* Rigadoon *Eng* (rig='wanton' in Shakespeare)

Nearly all the dances shown on the map on page 43 were brought to the court in the seventeenth century and soon became firm favourites. Only the rigaudon and the loure, however, are discussed in this chapter, for it is appropriate that the others (gavotte, passepied, bourrée and minuet) should appear in the chapter on the eighteenth century, in which they especially attracted the attention of the composers.

The rigaudon was a very lively leaping dance from Provence. Quite often it was based on this rhythmic pattern:

$\frac{2}{4}$ ♪ | ♫ ♫ | ♩.

although the up-beat quaver was not always a feature. It was extremely popular in England in the last twenty or so years of the century.

This is a rigaudon by the English composer PURCELL (1659–1695) who was the leading musician in the courts of Charles II, James II and William and Mary. Apart from his work for the court, Purcell also contributed music of the very highest quality for the stage, the Church, the home and the tavern. After his death his wife published his *Suites, Lessons and Pieces* for the harpsichord, which included this rigaudon.

More recent versions of the rigaudon are contained in Grieg's *Holberg Suite* and Ravel's *Le Tombeau de Couperin*.

Project 16

The tune of this rigaudon is particularly suited to performance on the recorder (descant or treble). When you have learnt to play it, try to add a number of variations of your own. More experienced musicians might make an arrangement for recorder ensemble.

Loure *Fr* (16th C.=bagpipe)

Like a number of other dances, the loure is named after the instruments which normally accompanied it in its peasant days, in Normandy. It was usually in triple time with this basic rhythm:

but often appeared in ⁶₈ as two ³₄ bars joined together:

Frontispiece from a 1713 printed edition of the opera *Armide* by Lully

The following example is taken from Lully's opera ALCESTE, which was first performed in 1674. The composer was the chief musician at Louis XIV's court at Versailles until his death in 1687.

Project 17
The key of this piece is G major. What proportion of time is the G major chord

50

used, and how much is the D major chord used? What other harmonies are used?

Canaries Canario *Sp*

The canaries was a dance imported from the Canary Islands and popular in Spain and France in the seventeenth century. It was a fairly lively dance, in some ways similar to the gigue (see page 88). It usually started on the first beat and the following rhythm is characteristic:

It was popular with the French clavecinists in particular, but it was also known in England, and a fine example occurs in Purcell's *Dioclesian*. The following example is taken from the *First Book of Pieces* by the French composer CHAM-BONNÈIRES (1602–1672), court harpsichordist to Louis XIV.

Project 18

Make a detailed analysis of this extract.

Bergamesca *It* (from the Bergamo region of northern Italy)

Although this dance is not as well known as many of the other dances of the seventeenth century, it was nevertheless very popular in its time. Of particular interest is the fact that, like the passamezzo, the bergamesca is essentially a series of chords over which a melody could be improvised. The chord sequence was much simpler than the passamezzo, however, and consisted of just the chords I, IV, V and I.

Here is an example by the German composer SCHEIDT (1587–1654), a pupil of the great Dutch composer Sweelinck. You will notice that the four chords are repeated every two bars, and that new melodic ideas are introduced with each variation. The whole piece is, of course, very much longer.

Project 19
With the instrument that you have available, improvise a number of melodies over the simple bass line. When you are satisfied with a set of such improvisations, try to write them down.

Review of the seventeenth century

Music in the Church	Italy	France	Germany Austria	England	Others
Vocal					
Mass, Motet	Carissimi	Lully	Buxtehude	Blow	Sweelinck
Service	Cavalli	Campra	Praetorius	Humfrey	(Dutch)
Anthem	Cesti		Schütz	Purcell	
Cantata	Frescobaldi		Scheidemann	Tomkins	
Oratorio	Monteverdi		Scheidt		
Requiem	Scarlatti, A.		Schein		
Passion					
Chorale					

Instrumental	Italy	France	Germany Austria	England	Others
Toccata					
Fantasia					
Prelude					
Fugue					
Canzona					
Ricercar					
Chorale					
Prelude					

Music in the Theatre					
Opera	Carissimi	Lully		Blow	
(Oratorio)	Cavalli	Campra		Humfrey	
Ballet	Cesti			Purcell	
Masque	Landi				
Overture	Monteverdi				
	Scarlatti, A.				

Music at the Court					
Ode	Corelli	Chambonnières	Froberger	Blow	
Masque		Couperin, L.	Buxtehude	Purcell	
Concerto		Lully	Praetorius	Humfrey	
			Schütz		
			Scheidemann		
			Scheidt		
			Schein		

Music in the Home (*other than dance music*)					
Sonata a 2,	Corelli	Chambonnières	Froberger	(Blow)	
3, 4, etc.	Frescobaldi	Couperin, L.	Buxtehude	(Gibbons)	
Canzona	Torelli	Lully	Pachelbel	(Byrd)	
Ricercar	Vitali	D'Anglebert	Scheidemann	(Coperario)	
Fantasia		Gaultier	Scheidt	(Dowland)	
Concerto			Schein	(Farnaby)	
Madrigal				(Weelkes)	
Song				(Wilbye)	
				Lawes Locke	
				Purcell	
				Tomkins	
				Jenkins	
				Simpson	

53

Revision Questions

1 Who wrote
   (*a*) *The English Dancing Master?*
   (*b*) *A choice collection of 8 lessons?*
   (*c*) *Dances for the lute?*
   (*d*) *Dioclesian?*
2 What is
   (*a*) a ricercar?
   (*b*) Les Vingt-quatre violins du Roy?
   (*c*) the ballet de cour?
   (*d*) a masque?
3 Why is/are
   (*a*) the 'canaries' so named?
   (*b*) the sarabande connected with America?
   (*c*) the date of the first edition of *The English Dancing Master* important?
   (*d*) the bergamesca so named?
4 What are the most important characteristics of
   (*a*) the courante?
   (*b*) corrento?
   (*c*) sarabande?
   (*d*) allemande?
5 Which are the most important countries, musically speaking, in the seventeenth
   century?

above Maria Theresa, 1740–1780
left Frederick II (the Great) of Prussia,
1712–1786

The Eighteenth Century

Compared with the previous century, at first sight the eighteenth century appears to be a period of comparative stability. Prussia and Austria settled down to an era of steady rule under, respectively, Frederick the Great (1740–86) and Maria Theresa (1740–80), despite the fact that they were involved in a series of prolonged conflicts with other European powers. France tottered through the reigns of Louis XIV, XV, and XVI almost permanently locked in conflict with Britain, and nevertheless managed to maintain some sort of leading role in Europe. In Britain the Hanoverian kings (George 1, II, III) did little to upset the increasing power of Parliament, led by a series of strong Prime Ministers (Walpole, the Pitts, Pelham and North). Britain's island position made the impact of the overseas wars (Canada, India, Europe) far less pronounced than it might otherwise have been.

In an increasingly prosperous atmosphere British craftsmen, scientists, inventors, painters and writers consolidated the achievements of the late seventeenth century.

C

The Library, Mellerstain, Kelso in Scotland, designed by Robert Adam, 1728–1792

The ceiling of the Music Room, Mellerstain, designed by Robert Adam

Eight medallions in Jasper ware, blue with white figures in relief, showing the seven muses and also Apollo. Designed by John Flaxman for Josiah Wedgewood about 1785

Chair designed by George Hepplewhite 1786

Cut-glass scent bottle with Jasper medallion, designed for Josiah Wedgewood

Lymington Iron Works on the Tyne

James Hargreaves's Spinning Jenny

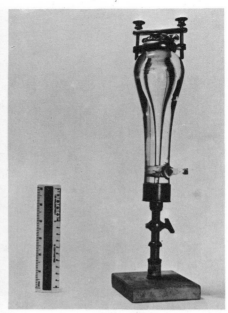

Henry Cavendish's endiometer which was designed to measure the volume of gases

James Watt's steam engine, *Puffing Billy*

Sectional view of Watt's engine

Johnathan Swift, 1667–1745   Alexander Pope, from a painting in
the Fitzwilliam Museum, 1688–1744

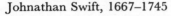

Adam, Hepplewhite, Wedgwood and others established standards of domestic craftsmanship which had few rivals in Europe. Cavendish and Priestley (chemists) led the British field in scientific discovery. Watt (steam engine), Crompton, Cartwright, and Hargreaves (textile machinery), Huntsman, Cort and Darby (heavy engineering) led the progress in industry. Gainsborough, Reynolds and Romney represented the best of British painting. Goldsmith, Sheridan, Adam Smith and Gibbon were among the leading writers; and eighteenth-century tendency towards complacency was counterbalanced by the work of the brilliant satirists Defoe, Swift, Pope and Johnson (writers) and Hogarth (painter).

The eighteenth century is often referred to as 'the Age of Enlightenment', a period in which the European leaders thought that they had arrived at a period of history when nothing stood in the way of great economic and social progress. Leading exponents of this idea were the French writers Voltaire and Rousseau, whose work had considerable influence throughout Europe.

But the cultivated surface of eighteenth-century life was shattered in the

60

Painting from the series *Marriage à la Mode* by William Hogarth, 1697–1764

closing years. The French Revolution (1789) and the American Revolution (1776) are but two of the many conflicts that brought the century of enlightenment to a rather violent close.

Nevertheless, the atmosphere of enquiry by now had been so successfully established that the path of nineteenth century investigation was clearly determined. The appearance of a number of dictionaries (e.g. Johnson's) and encyclopaedias (e.g. Diderot's) is characteristic of this spirit of enquiry.

In both England and France this general demand for information is illustrated in the particular demand for information about dancing. In the eighteenth century the widening public interest is confirmed by the appearance of a number of books on the subject. The growing middle classes (especially in England) could content themselves with the written advice of the court dancing masters where they could not obtain it at first hand.

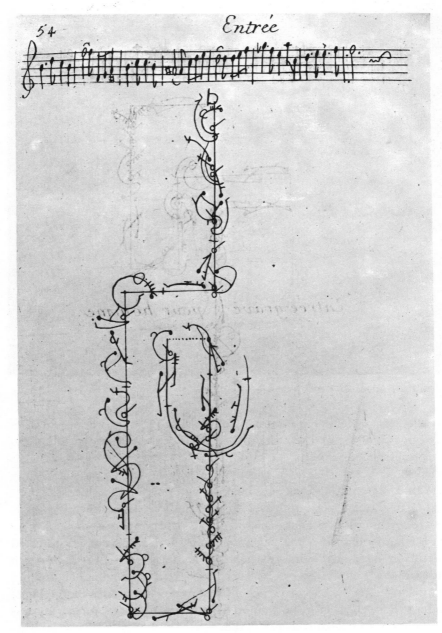

Illustration from *Chorégraphie* by Feuillet, published in 1701

Table des Pirouettes.

ouvrir la Iambe et la croiser derriere, pour pirouetter sur les 2. pointes des pieds, demy tour.

ouvrir la Iambe et la croiser devant, pour pirouetter sur les 2. pointes des pieds, demy tour

pirouette ouvert^e demy tour en dehors.

ouverte, demy tour en dedans.

ouvert^e un tour en dehors.

ouvert^e un tour en dedans

ouverte vn tour en dehors.

ouvert^e vn tour en dedans.

ouvert^e un tour et demy en dehors

ouvert^e un tour et demy en dedans

Illustrations from *Chorégraphie* by Feuillet, published in 1701

63

Illustration from *Le Maître de Danser* by P. Rameau, published in 1734

In France two figures are particularly important. R. A. FEUILLET was one of the first writers to work out a system for setting down the actual dance steps in diagrams. His book *Choréographie* was written in the first years of the century, and was imitated by several other writers. In 1725, P. RAMEAU, who was 'Dancing Master to the Pages of Her Catholic Majesty, the Queen of Spain' (and *not* the composer Jean-Philippe Rameau) wrote *The Dancing Master*, a book which had considerable influence.

The following selection of English publications gives some indication of the widespread interest in dancing in the early years of the century:

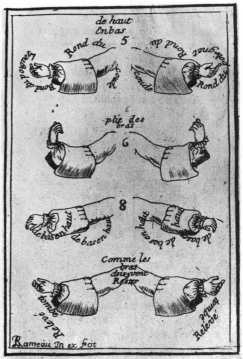

Representation des mouvements des poignets Coudes et de l'épaule

Deuxieme attitude des saillies

Illustrations from *Le Maître de Danser* by P. Rameau, published in 1734

1706 WEAVER, *The Art of Dancing* (tr. from Feuillet)
1710 ESSEX, *For the Further Improvement of Dancing* (tr. from Feuillet)
1711 PEMBERTON, *An Essay for the Further Improvement of Dancing*
1712 WEAVER, *Essay towards an History of Dancing*
1729 JENYNS, *The Art of Dancing*
1735 TOMLINSON, *The Art of Dancing*
1738 BICKHAM, *An Easy Introduction to Dancing*

Combined with this interest in dancing was, of course, the continued demand for dance music that could be played at home by the amateur musician. The

Illustration from *The Art of Dancing* by Kellom Tomlinson, published in 1735

Illustration from *The Art of Dancing* by Kellom Tomlinson, published in 1735

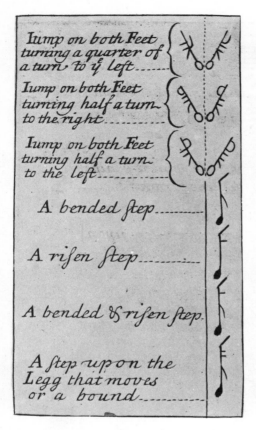

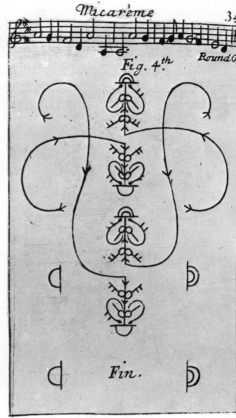

Illustrations from *For the Further Improvement of Dancing* by **Essex**, published in 1710

Johann Sebastian Bach, 1685–1750

suite, therefore, remained a popular form of instrumental music. To the older dances of the early seventeenth century were added the newer dances of Louis XIV's court. The allemande, courante and sarabande were followed by one or more of the gavottes, bourrées, minuets or other French dances, and the suite was completed in the high spirits of the gigue.

At least this was the pattern most favoured by J. S. BACH (1685–1750) whose sets of six English Suites, six French Suites, and six Partitas, for keyboard, and four Suites for orchestra, are perhaps the most well known examples of instrumental dances in the history of music. By Bach's time the practice of beginning the suite with a prelude before the allemande was quite common, and thus the whole suite would generally contain at least six movements. (Mnemonic: P – A – C – S –O (others) – G='pacsog'.) Moreover many of the dances were accompanied by one or more variations (doubles). German contemporaries of Bach who contributed many entertaining suites were:

Muffat G. (1690–1770), Telemann (1681–1767), Mattheson (1681–1764), Böhm (1661–1733), Fischer (1665–1746), Kuhnau (1660–1722)

François Couperin, 1668–1733

In France the 'ordre' (suite) was not so carefully organised. Although the general scheme might be similar, very often the ordre was simply a string of dances without any special pattern, treated as isolated movements and not as the grand structure of the German suite. Moreover, most of the dances were given descriptive titles rather than actual dance names. FRANCOIS COUPERIN 'Le Grand' (1668–1733) and JEAN-PHILIPPE RAMEAU (1683–1764) were the leading clavecinists to write such pieces.

Couperin's four books of clavecin pieces were written between 1710 and 1730. Sometimes an *ordre* would include just four or five dances and on other occasions as many as twenty. Rameau's three books date from 1706, and contain most of the traditional forms.

DOMENICO SCARLATTI (1685–1757), son of the famous operatic composer Alessandro Scarlatti, was the leading Italian keyboard composer of the period. Although he was born in Naples (and met Handel in Rome) he spent most of his working life in Spain. He wrote at least six hundred one-movement sonatas, which although far less tied to the dance than some of those of his contemporaries, contain many pieces based on dance rhythms. VIVALDI (1675–1741) is known chiefly for his violin concertos, but he wrote a considerable number of sonatas for two violins and continuo which contained allemandes, courantes,

George Frederick Handel, 1685–1759

sarabandes, gavottes and gigues (although the order of dances never followed the 'German' pattern.)

HANDEL is the sixth great name in the instrumental dance forms of the first half of the eighteenth century (Bach, Couperin, Rameau, Scarlatti, Vivaldi). His choice of dances is mainly German in pattern, although he did include such unconventional forms as the chaconne, passacaglia, hornpipe and siciliano. It is interesting to imagine how important as a writer of dance music Purcell might have been if he had not died so early. If he had lived as many years as Bach, for example (i.e. until 1723) he would no doubt have become the seventh member of this illustrious group. As it was, English music did not have a composer of similar status for nearly two hundred years.

In the second half of the century the Germans and Austrians were almost the only serious contenders for the leading position in European instrumental music. Both France and Italy seemed to have become submerged in opera to an extent which stifled natural growth in any other fields of composition, and English composers disappeared into the dark tunnel from which they were not to emerge until the end of the nineteenth century. It is true that Paris established its famous series of orchestral concerts (*Concerts Spirituels*) during this time, but only GOSSEC (1734–1829) offered any real alternative to imported instrumental

F

Franz Joseph Haydn, 1732–1809

music. In Italy only BOCCHERINI (1743–1805) maintained the instrumental tradition.

The foundations of the 'symphonic' style were established in Germany by a group of composers, chief among whom were C. P. E. BACH (1714–1788), second son of J. S. B., in Berlin and Hamburg, and C. STAMITZ (1745–1801), in Mannheim. They were followed by two of the most important symphonists, HAYDN (1732–1809) and MOZART (1756–1791). Practically the only survivor of the transformation of the suite to the symphony was the minuet, which very quickly became the customary choice for the third movement of the four movement symphony (quick-slow-minuet-quick).

Although interest in other dance forms had not been completely abandoned, nevertheless it is generally true to say that by the end of the century only the minuet and the country dances remained popular in the ballroom, and since the country dances were often based simply on collections of popular tunes of the day, and not on any particular musical ideas, then we are left with the minuet as the only dance form of real influence. What an amazing contrast with the beginning of the century!

Wolfgang Amadeus Mozart, 1756–1791

Minuet (menuet) *Fr* menu = small (steps) minuetto *It*

The minuet is probably the most famous dance in the history of instrumental music. Alone among the dances of the early eighteenth century suite it survived in the new surroundings of the symphony.

It had originally been introduced to the court of Louis XIV (in about 1650) as a popular dance from the Poitou area. It became a firm favourite at Versailles, and quickly spread throughout the courts of Europe. Of the many local dances which had reached the court during Louis's reign, it was the only one that maintained its popularity until the close of the century.

In the atmosphere of the court, the minuet gradually lost its Poitou roughness (where it was probably a descendant of the branle) and became the supreme example of the graceful court fashions. It demanded a considerable sense of balance and control, and was often regarded as a test of a person's ability to conduct himself well in public.

In the four-movement symphony of the second half of the century, the minuet usually occupied the third position, providing a graceful link between the serious slow movement and the light-hearted finale. The main minuet was almost always followed by a second, shorter, minuet, usually called the TRIO

73

(deriving its name from an early practice of writing the second minuet for a group of only three instruments). The Trio was then followed by a repeat of the first minuet, giving the following structure:

Minuet 1 (in binary form both sections repeated),

Trio (*Minuet 2*) (in binary form, both sections repeated)

Minuet 1 (without the repeats)

The minuets of the late Mozart and Haydn symphonies often acquired the dramatic atmosphere of the other movements of the symphony, and conveyed a very different feeling from that of the gracious dances of the early part of the century. In due course these vigorous third movements were given the name 'scherzo' which more appropriately described their purpose.

HAYDN *Minuet*

Menuetto da capo

This minuet is a movement from a piano sonata by HAYDN (1732–1809). He and Mozart were the leading composers of the end of the eighteenth century. For most of his life Haydn worked for the Esterhazy family, one of the richest and most famous families in the whole of Europe. His time was spent producing music of all types – for the theatre, the chapel and the concert room – in the castle of Eisenstadt, the palace of Esterhazy or in the town house in Vienna. Modern versions can be found in Ravel's *Sonatine* and *Le Tombeau de Couperin*.

Project 20

Make a detailed analysis of this movement, and compare it with any other minuets that you may have studied.

Passepied *Fr* Pass-foot or paspy *Eng*

The passepied is similar in some ways to the minuet. Both dances arrived at Versailles about 1650; both are in a moderate three beat tempo (although the passepied may be a little quicker); both originate from branles of N.W. France,

75

the passepied coming from Brittany. It is therefore rather strange that the one should be so much more famous than the other.

The name 'pass-foot' refers to the characteristic step of the dance in which one foot crosses over the other. Unlike the minuet, the passepied usually begins on the third beat of the bar, the preliminary up-beat being a feature of the steps. Perhaps the numerous minuets which begin on the up-beat should really be called 'passepied and trio'? Here is an example of a passepied by Bach.

BACH Fifth English Suite *Passepied en Rondeau*

Project 21

Make a detailed analysis of this movement.

Gavotte *Fr* (Gavots=people of the Pays de Gap in Upper Dauphiné)
Although this dance was mentioned by Arbeau (*Orchésographie* 1588) and was
well known throughout the seventeenth century, it has been allocated to the
dances of the eighteenth century because so many fine examples were written at
that time.

This is the characteristic rhythm:

in moderate tempo.

The feet were lifted and not shuffled as in the minuet. In the suite it was often
coupled with a second gavotte containing a drone bass, and this was called a
MUSETTE (small bagpipe).

Roger North, whose writings on music provide us with a great deal of information about the early eighteenth century, states that 'Gavotts, Courants, Giggs
and the like, are calculated for merry feasting and dancing . . .'

F. COUPERIN Gavotte *Les Moissonneurs*

Project 22

Make up a gavotte melody using this rhythm:

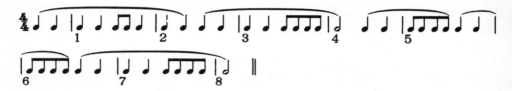

Bourrée *Fr* Borry *Eng*

Although the bourrée had its origins in southern France it was probably more popular in Germany, at least as far as its appearances in suites is concerned. The characteristic features are:

Quick **4/4** or ¢ ♩ | ♩ ♫ ♩ ♩ | ♩ ♫ ♩

In the French court it was seen mostly in the ballets (Lully), but it did not acquire the fame of some of the other French peasant dances. It was, however, well known in England at the beginning of the century.

J. S. BACH Second English Suite *Bourrée 1*

82

55

Project 23
Make up a bourrée melody using this rhythm:

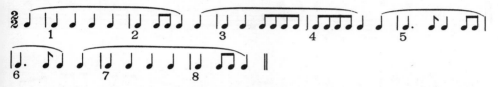

Country Dance Contre Danse *Fr* Kontretanz *Ger*

With most of the dances that we have met so far in this book the English have produced versions of foreign words that as near as possible suggest the sound of the originals. But with the country dance, the position is reversed. The French changed country into 'contre' understandably enough. But when the Germans took up the dance they assumed the 'contre' referred to type of formations that often occurred, that is, one line *against* (contre) another. Curiously, some German versions were brought back to this country and were known as ' contra ' by those who thought the German word sounded grander than the original English.

Country dances had originally become popular in England during the reign of Elizabeth, and had maintained great popularity throughout the seventeenth century. But, as has been pointed out in the previous chapter, the country dance never really established itself as an instrumental form. But the German *contratanz* was a different matter, and it appeared as an instrumental form at the end of the century. In France, where it rivalled the minuet in popularity, it was also known as the *Française*, and later as the *cotill(i)on* and the *quadrille*.

Kellom Tomlinson supplies us with some interesting observations on the country dance in his book *The Art of Dancing* (1735):

'Tho' my original design was only to have spoke of genteel *Dancing* yet as *Country Dances* are at all *Assemblies* or *Balls* introduced as it were a part of or belonging to the former ... and is becoming as it were the *Darling* or favourite

Diversion of all Ranks of People from the Court to the Cottage . . . I shall . . . endeavour to point out those *Neglects* which render this Diversion much less pleasant . . .'

Here is an example by MOZART (1756–1791):

Siciliano *It* (=from Sicily) Sicilienne *Fr*

The siciliano rhythm is a rather graceful and flowing $\frac{6}{8}$ or $\frac{12}{8}$ which was often used by seventeenth- and eighteenth-century composers without reference to the actual dance by name. It occurs quite often in the works of Corelli, Couperin Rameau and Bach, but it is particularly characteristic of the music of DOMENICO SCARLATTI (1685–1757) whose father was born in Sicily.

Part of a sonata by Scarlatti is given on the opposite page.

87

Project 24
Make a detailed analysis of this music.

Gigue *Fr* Giga *It* Jig *Eng*

The origin of the gigue is uncertain, but it is possibly named after a medieval stringed instrument. The dance was well known in the Elizabethan court, and popular with Louis XIV, but it did not really establish itself in the suite until the end of the seventeenth century, and it was left to the early eighteenth century masters to give it its most powerful forms of expression. To Bach, Handel, Rameau and Couperin the gigue was not simply a light-hearted romp at the end of the suite, but the opportunity to display dramatically many of the contrapuntal fireworks in their possession.

As with the courante, we can recognise a typically French and a typically Italian type of gigue. The French style is more dramatic, with dotted rhythms and wide intervals, while the Italian style is more flowing and simple. Compare these two openings from Bach suites:

French style:

Italian style:

Most of Bach's gigues are in a contrapuntal style with two or three parts closely imitatating each other. This example by Rameau, however, is in a much simpler style. Do you think it would be called a French gigue or an Italian one?

RAMEAU *Gigue en Rondeau*

Project 25

Explain fully why Rameau calls this a '*Gigue en Rondeau*'?

Hornpipe *Eng*

This dance is named after an early woodwind instrument which was probably commonly used for the accompaniment. The dance was popular in England from the sixteenth to the nineteenth century, and was generally known as a country dance long before it became associated with the folded arms sailors' dance of the nineteenth century. The eighteenth-century version was usually in $\frac{3}{2}$ rhythm, and although it was very popular in England it did reach the continent as well. Here is an example by the German composer GOTTLIEB MUFFAT (1690–1770):

MUFFAT *Hornpipe*

Project 26

Write a hornpipe melody for any instruments that you have available.

Chaconne and Passacaglia

These two dances are musically so similar that it is almost impossible to differentiate between them. Like the basse dance, the passamezzo and others, the chaconne and the passacaglia contain a repeated bass figure over which melodic parts are improvised or written. The chaconne takes its name from a Mexican dance imported into Spain in the early seventeenth century. The English called it the 'chacony'. The passacaglia either means 'street song' or 'street step' and is again associated with Spain.

Perhaps more than any other dances the chaconne and passacaglia very quickly became removed from their origin as dances, and became the most familiar ground-bass structures of the seventeenth and eighteenth centuries.

The famous organ passacaglias of Bach, with their majestic, slow moving basses are only related very distantly to the world of the dance.

Here is the opening of passacaglia for harpsichord by HANDEL (1685–1759). In all it contains sixteen variations.

No.2

Project 27
Write one or more variations of this passacaglia of your own invention.

Review of the eighteenth century

Music in the Church	Italy	France	Germany Austria	England
Mass, Service Passion Cantata Anthem Motet Oratorio	Marcello Piccini	Gossec Campra	Bach J.S. Bach C.P.E. Mozart Haydn	Handel
Music in the Theatre Opera (Ballet)	Cimarosa Pergolesi Scarlatti A Piccini	Campra Gluck Rameau Gretry	Graun Mozart Haydn Hasse (Gluck)	Handel Arne
Music in the Concert Hall Symphony Concerto Serenade	Corelli Vivaldi Geminiani Sammartini Boccherini	Gossec	Bach J.S. Bach C.P.E. (Bach J.C.) Mozart Haydn Stamitz Telemann Dittersdorf	Handel Bach J.C. Boyce Arne
Music in the Home (*other than dance music*) Sonata (solo) Sonata for two instruments Trios, Quartets etc. Songs	Corelli Scarlatti D Vivaldi Germiniani Boccherini	Couperin, F. Rameau Gossec	Bach J.S. Bach C.P.E. (Bach J.C.) Quantz Kuhnau Mozart Haydn Telemann	Handel Bach J.C.

Revision Questions

1 Who wrote
   (a) *The Dancing Master?*
   (b) *Choréographie?*
   (c) *The Decline and Fall of the Roman Empire?*
   (d) an important English dictionary?
2 What is/are
   (a) 'Concerts Spirituels'?
   (b) the 'branle de Poitou'?
   (c) the 'paspy'?
   (d) the Kontretantz?
3 Why is/are
   (a) the musette so named?
   (b) the gigue and courante similar?
   (c) the suite less important in the second half of the century?
   (d) the country dances comparatively unimportant as far as the composers are concerned?
4 What are the most important characteristics of the
   (a) minuet?
   (b) gavotte?
   (c) bourrée?
   (d) gigue?
5 Which are the most important countries, musically speaking, in the eighteenth century?

The United States Mail steam ship *Atlantic* entering the Mersey in 1850

The Nineteenth Century

The nineteenth century not only saw political revolutions in a number of European countries, but also the economic and social revolution that we call the Industrial Revolution. The railways, steamships, telegraph, telephone and electricity were only a few of the many new features of nineteenth-century life.

Britain now commanded a powerful empire abroad, and a powerful industrial growth at home. Both Germany and Italy at last became unified countries. France slowly recovered from the disasters of the Revolution, and by the end of the century had almost regained the artistic leadership in Europe that it had lost in the eighteenth century. The countries of eastern Europe and Scandinavia now began to take a much more important part in the cultural life of Europe, and the work of Russian, Bohemian and Hungarian artists in particular became familiar throughout Europe.

In music German and Austrian composers continued to dominate the scene for most of the century, maintaining the concerto, symphony, sonata, quartet, song and opera as their chief means of expression, but re-establishing dance forms (especially for the piano) as an important part of the repertoire. Italian music continued to be almost entirely absorbed in opera, and this was generally true of French music also, although there was a considerable growth in other forms towards the end of the century. A great injection of new ideas came from those countries surrounding the old triangle of France, Germany and Italy, and dance forms from eastern Europe and Spain became very popular in all the capital cities.

The general position of dancing in the early part of the century is well illustrated in a book published in England in 1816 by Thomas Wilson, 'Dancing Master from the King's Theatre Opera House'. In his *Companion to the Ball Room* he suggests on more than one occasion that the standards of dancing were not as high as they might have been. A criticism of the dancers:

'Few Tunes of this Measure ($\frac{9}{8}$) are to be found in Collections of Country Dances; and the reason is, those who are indifferent Dancers, and are not acquainted with proper steps (a class of people in which Ball Rooms usually abound) would find great difficulty in performing them.'

is followed by comments on the musicians:

'The times of the Dances (although properly the province of the Musician) ought likewise to be known to the Dancers themselves, that they may be enabled to correct any Error arising from the misunderstanding or inattention of the Band or other causes, and to prevent them being thrown into confusion, by the Errors or Presumption of others.'

If the position in England was similar to that in other parts of Europe, then it is probable that dancing was no longer generally regarded as an activity that demands the constant practice and attention to detail that had been a feature of dancing during most of the previous three centuries.

The dances that captured the attention of the ballroom public were the waltz and the polka as couple dances, and reels, hornpipes, quadrilles, cotillons and country dances as group dances. And as Wilson points out, the group dances did not attract the composers:

'The only reason to be assigned why collections of Country Dances have been so deficient both in Merit and Originality, is that good Composers have considered that it would not pay them for composing Dances as the Publishers cannot afford anything like, what may be termed a Price, since they have got into the method of selling twenty-four *new dances* for a shilling ...'

Therefore the waltz and to a very smaller extent the polka, are the only generally popular dances which interested the composer. To these may be added the Austrian Ländler (a living ancestor of the waltz), the mazurka and polonaise

Ludwig van Beethoven, 1770–1827

from Poland, the tarantella and saltarello from Italy, and a few new dances from the areas we would now call Czechoslovakia and Hungary.

As will have been noticed, dance forms are especially appropriate for short pieces of music. The characteristic nineteenth century instrumental forms are, however, large ones like the movements of the symphony or the concerto. It is not surprising therefore, that dances take a less important role than they did in previous centuries. Nevertheless, most composers used dances in at least one of three ways:

1 The 'new' dances as separate instrumental pieces for the concert platform or the home, e.g. Chopin: waltzes, mazurkas and polonaises; Brahms: waltzes and *Hungarian Dances;* Dvořák: *Slavonic Dances.*

2 The 'old' dances either as a natural part of the symphony or sonata (e.g. minuet) or as a deliberate revival of 'historical' dances, e.g. Grieg's *Holberg Suite,* Debussy's *Suite Bergamasque,* Fauré's *Pavane* and Saint-Saëns's *Pavane* from the ballet *Etienne Marcel.*

3 Movements in symphonies (etc.) that derive their rhythmic impetus from dances without consciously setting out to imitate them, e.g. Beethoven's 6/iii, 7/ii, 9/ii, Brahm's 4/iv, Dvořák's 8/iii, iv.

Franz Schubert, 1797–1828

Waltz Waltzer *Ger* Valse *Fr* valzero (or danza tedesca) *It*
The waltz was easily the most popular dance of the nineteenth century, and of course is still very popular today. It probably derived from the Austrian Ländler which was a somewhat slower dance performed outdoors in heavier shoes. The waltz concentrates on gliding steps and therefore demands smooth ball-room floors, lighter shoes and slightly quicker steps. The dancers also turn in circles as they progress down the ballroom and this revolving movement (*Lat* volvere) is probably responsible for its name.

The dance required the couples to hold each other throughout, and at first attracted a certain amount of opposition from the more conservative circles. In Reese's *Cyclopaedia* (1805), an article by the famous English music historian, Dr Charles Burney, states: 'having seen it performed by a select party of foreigners, we could not help reflecting how uneasy an English mother would be to see her daughter so familiarly treated.'

Nevertheless it soon became the most popular dance in Europe, and was in great demand as pieces to be played at home or in the concert hall. Here is a short list of some of the most famous waltzes of the nineteenth century:

BEETHOVEN   33 *Variations on a waltz by Diabelli, Op* 120 (1823)

Johannes Brahms, 1833–1897

SCHUBERT   12 *Gratzer Waltzer, Op* 91 (1827)
WEBER   *Invitation to the Dance* (1819)
CHOPIN   Waltzes (1826–1848)
STRAUSS J.   from the opera *Die Fledermaus* (1874)
LISZT   *Mephisto Waltz* (1880)
·BERLIOZ   *Symphonie Fantastique, Op* 14 (1831)
TCHAIKOVSKY *Fifth Symphony* (*Op* 64 1888) and ballets (e,g. *Sleeping Beauty*)
BRAHMS   *Liebeslieder Waltzer, Op* 52 (1869)
DVOŘÁK   Waltzes, *Op* 54 (1880)

Here is a waltz written by Brahms (*Op* 39 no. 11):

Project 28

Write a simple waltz tune over this bass:

G   C   D   G   Emin   C   D7   G

Mazurka *Polish*

The mazurka was a popular song and dance of the seventeenth century which spread to Prussian court circles in the eighteenth century, and to the concert platform in the nineteenth, chiefly through the work of Chopin, who was himself born in the region around Warsaw from which the dance originated.

Although the mazurka has the same time signature as the waltz, it is easy to distinguish with its dotted rhythms and accented weak beats:

The example is the *Mazurka in G minor* (*Op* 24) by Chopin.

Project 29

Write a simple 8 bar mazurka melody in A minor.

Polka *Czech*

This dance first became popular in Prague in about 1835, and quickly spread
to all parts of Europe. It was a lively dance in $\frac{2}{4}$ time, and made a useful contrast to the waltz. It seems somehow to have got confused with a Scottish
country dance, for the Germans sometimes called the polka the 'Schottische'
and the French the 'écossaise'. The most famous examples are by the Czech
composers SMETANA (1824–84) and DVOŘÁK (1841–1904).

Although alternative rhythms have been used, the most common pattern is
the following:

The GALOP is a quicker version of the polka.

The polka on the following page by Dvorák, although not based exactly on
the above rhythm, is an interesting example of the type.

Antonin Dvořák, 1841–1904

Project 30
Write a polka melody of about eight bars for any available instruments.

Tarantella and Saltarello
These are two Italian dances which were popular in the nineteenth century in Italy, and were used on a number of occasions by composers who wanted to suggest an Italian flavour.

The $\begin{smallmatrix}6\\8\end{smallmatrix}$ rhythm is common to both, and the tempo is quick in both cases, which makes them difficult to distinguish. The tarantella comes from the south of Italy and is probably named after the town of Taranto. There is, however, a more colourful explanation: namely, that the dance was a cure for the bite of the deadly tarantula spider! The saltarello (saltare=to jump) was popular in the Rome area. The saltarello had been known earlier in the sixteenth century as one of the triple metre dances connected with the basse dance and the passamezzo. The nineteenth century version was, however, much more violent.

The most famous example of the use of these dance rhythms occurs in the last movement of Mendelssohn's *Fourth Symphony, The Italian.*

Review of the nineteenth century

Music in the Church	*Italy*	*France*	*Germany Austria*	*Russia*	*Others*
Mass	Verdi	Berlioz	Beethoven		Stanford
Service					(England)
Anthem					Parry
Oratorio					(England)
(often concert hall music)					
Music in the Theatre					
Opera	Verdi	Berlioz	Weber	Balakirev	Dvořák
(Music	Rossini	Bizet	Wagner	Glazunov	(Bohemia)
Drama)	Puccini	Saint-Saëns	Meyerbeer	Glinka	Smetana
Ballet	Donizetti	Delibes	Strauss J.	Rimsky-	(Bohemia)
Plays with	Bellini	Auber		Korsakov	
music	Charubini	Chabrier		Mussorgsky	
		Massenet		Tchaikovsky	
		Halévy			
Music in the Concert Hall					
Symphony		Berlioz	Beethoven	Tchaikovsky	Dvořák
Concerto		Frank	Schubert	Rimsky-	(Bohemia)
Overture		Saint-Saëns	Schumann	Korsakov	Grieg
Tone Poem		Debussy	Mendelssohn	Mussorgsky	(Norway)
Variations		Indy	Brahms		Lizst
Suite (not			Bruckner		(Hungary)
dance suite)			Mahler		

Music in the Home (other than dance music)	Italy	France	Germany Austria	Russia	Others
Sonata (solo piano) Sonata (e.g. violin & piano) Trio, Quartet, etc. Song, Lieder		Chausson Frank Indy Debussy Fauré	Beethoven Schubert Schumann Mendelssohn Brahms Wolf	Tchaikovsky Mussorgsky	Chopin (Paris) Grieg (Norway) Lizst (Hungary) Field (England) Clementi (England)

Revision Questions

1 Who wrote
 (a) *Symphonie Fantastique?*
 (b) *the Italian symphony?*
 (c) *Invitation to the dance?*
 (d) *Companion to the Ballroom?*

2 What is a
 (a) Ländler?
 (b) Schottische?
 (c) Polacca?

3 Why is the
 (a) Waltz particularly popular in Vienna?
 (b) Waltz the most popular dance of the nineteenth century?
 (c) general influence of the dance on instrumental music less strong in the nineteenth century?
 (d) influence of countries in eastern Europe important in this century?

4 What are the most important characteristics of the
 (a) Waltz?
 (b) Mazurka?
 (c) Polonaise?
 (d) Polka?

5 Which are the most important countries, musically speaking, in the nineteenth century?

The Twentieth Century

As far as music is concerned, the two most important factors in the twentieth century have been the development of the means of mass communication – newpapers, radio, television, the gramophone and the cinema, and the increase in the amount of leisure time available to a very great number of people.

The ease with which music can be obtained has both advantages and disadvantages. There can be no doubt that today the composer can reach a far wider audience than was ever possible before, and that for the first time many people have easy access to the best music of at least the last four hundred years. But unfortunately, this easy access has been accompanied by a marked laziness on the part of many people. Since it is possible to enjoy music by simply switching a knob, they say, why take all the bother of learning to be a musician oneself? Since it is very easy to enjoy listening to the familiar styles, why make the effort to investigate the unfamiliar?

The increase in leisure time has, curiously enough, also produced problems. At first it may seem strange that people should not know how to enjoy their freedom from the labours of the factory and the office, but for many it has meant hours of boredom and perhaps loneliness.

Fortunately an increasingly large number of people have found that personally taking part in performances not only increases their enjoyment of music, but also brings them into contact with with a wider circle of friends. In Britain, for example, the number of amateur choirs, orchestras, bands, groups and ensembles of every description is enormous. So also is the number of people who now go to concerts in order to compare their own efforts with those of the professionals.

Nevertheless the first half of the twentieth century saw a horrifying situation develop. Supplied with a vast quantity of music, the only purpose of which was to make a quick profit for the businessman (whose only interest in music was financial), the general public rapidly lost contact with what the genuine composer was trying to do. At the same time the composer found it more and more difficult to discover any point of contact with those sections of the public that only wanted 'easy' entertainment. The result has been a partial breakdown in the natural flow of ideas between the composer and the public.

The relationship between dancing and music is a particularly clear example of this breakdown. In each of the previous four centuries, the composer has turned to the dances popular at the time and found in them a great source of inspiration. Indeed it is not an exaggeration to say that some of the best music of the past has sprung directly from the impact of dance rhythms on the composer's imagination. But with only a few exceptions, the twentieth century composer has found that the modern dance hall has nothing to offer him. Of the hundreds of 'new' dances only the South American rumba and tango rhythms have had any recognisable influence, and that was very slight.

Project 31

The RUMBA belongs to the 'ground-bass' type, e.g.:

over which fairly extended rhapsodic melodies can be made. Improvise some melodies over the rumba rhythm. Write down the best of them.

Project 32

The TANGO has a number of different forms, e.g.:

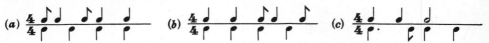

Tangos are mostly in the MINOR key. Write Tangos for (a) piano, or (b) two guitars, or (c) an instrumental group of your own choice.

Project 33

The FOXTROT consists basically of a mixture of $\frac{3}{4}$ and $\frac{4}{4}$ rhythms, e.g.:

Clap some foxtrot rhythms, and when you have got the feeling of them, improvise some melodies.

Project 34

Try to work out some ideas from the really *latest* dances that you know. First make certain that you understand the rhythms employed, then study the type of melody and harmony used. Composers in the past have always gained ideas

112

from the popular dances of their time. There is no reason why you should not be inspired by the dances of your own generation.

Although they have generally ignored popular dances, nevertheless composers have continued to use dance rhythms in their music. In some cases the derivation is obvious: the folk dances from Hungary, for example, have played an important part in the music of Bartok and Kodály, and Russian dances in the music of Stravinsky, Prokofiev and Shostakovich; or composers have deliberately revived some of the dances of other centuries – the pavane, the minuet, or the waltz. But in other cases the dance influence is strong but indefinable, more the *feeling* of dance rhythms than the actual imitation of particular examples.

The following list of dance works provides an interesting introduction to the music of our own century. From time to time most of these pieces can be heard on the radio, and recordings of many of them are available. Try to make a 'collection' of those you have heard, and make a few brief notes on them to remind yourself of what you have heard.

N.B. This list includes some ballets. In the previous chapters ballet music has generally not been included as its department is really 'Music and the Theatre'. However, so many twentieth century scores are known as concert pieces rather than actual ballets that it has been thought appropriate to include them here.

BRITISH

Arnold (1921–)	8 *English Dances* / 4 *Scottish Dances*
Bliss (1891–)	*Suite for piano*
Bridge (1879–1931)	*Dance Rhapsody*
Britten (1913–)	*Courtly Dances (Gloriana)*
Delius (1862–1934)	*Dance Rhapsody*
Elgar (1857–1934)	*Wand of Youth, Suite* 1 *and* 2
Hamilton (1922–)	*Scottish Dances*
Holst (1874–1934)	*St Paul's Suite*
Lambert (1905–51)	*Rio Grande*
Tippett (1905–)	*Suite in D*
Vaughan Williams (1872–1958)	'*Job*' – *a masque for dancing*
Walton (1902–)	*Façade, Suites* 1 *and* 2
Warlock (1894–1930)	*Capriol Suite*

GERMAN/AUSTRIAN

Hindemith (1895–1963)	*Symphonic Dances*
Orff (1895–)	*Carmina Burana*

Schoenberg (1874–1951)	*Suite for Piano* (1925)
Strauss, R. (1864–1949)	*Der Rosenkavalier*

FRENCH

Debussy (1862–1918)	*Suite Bergamasque*
	Gigues (Images)
Fauré (1845–1924)	*Dolly Suite*
D'Indy (1851–1931)	*Suite for orchestra, Op.* 24
Honegger (1892–1955)	*Suite Jour de fête Suisse*
	Suite archaique
Martin (1890–)	*Suite for orchestra*
Milhaud (1892–)	*Suite Provençale*
	Suite Française
Poulenc (1899–1963)	*Suite Française*
Ravel (1875–1937)	*Bolero*
	Pavane pour une enfante défunte
	Le Tombeau de Couperin
Roussel (1869–1937)	*Suite in F for orchestra*

ITALIAN

Casella (1883–1947)	*Suite in C*
	11 Children's Pieces
Dallapiccola (1904 –)	*Partita for orchestra*
Pizzetti (1880–1969)	*Suite from Pisanella*

SPANISH

Falla (1876–1946)	*The Three-Cornered Hat*
Gerhard (1896–1970)	*Dances from Don Quixote*
Granados (1867–1916)	*Suite for orchestra*

RUSSIAN

Khachaturian (1903–)	*Dance suite for orchestra*
Prokofiev (1881–1953)	*Suite for orchestra*
Shostakovich (1906–)	*Suite for dance band*
Stravinsky (1882–)	*Petrouchka*
	Firebird
	Polka for Circus Elephants
	Dances concertantes

HUNGARIAN/CZECH
Bartók (1881–1945)

Dance suite
Suites 1 and 2
Dances from 'Mikrokosmos'
Rumanian folk dances
Dances in 'For Children'

Dohnányi (1877–1959)   *Suite 'Ruralia Hungarica'*
Kodály (1882–1967)   *Dances of Galanta*
Martinů (1890–1958)   *Partita for orchestra*
Janáček (1854–1928)   *Sinfonietta*

AMERICAN
Barber (1920–   )   *Serenade for string quartet*
Bernstein (1918–   )   *West Side Story*
Copland (1900—   )   *Dance Symphony*
Gershwin (1898–1937)   *Dances from ' Porgy and Bess '*
Piston (1894–   )   *Orchestral suites 1 and 2*
Thomson (1898–   )   *Two sentimental tangos (1923)*

OTHERS
Nielsen (1865–1931) Dannish   *Suite for piano*
Sibelius (1865–1957) Finnish   *Valse Triste*
Skalkottas (1904–1949) Greek   *Greek dances for orchestra*
Villa-Lobos (1887–1959) Brazilian   *Dances in 'Bachianas Brasilieras'*

Benjamin Britten

Gustav Holst

Ralph Vaughan Williams

Luigi Dallapiccola

Claude Debussy

Paul Hindemith

117

Igor Stravinsky

Béla Bartók

Manuel de Falla

Zoltán Kodály

Aaron Copland

Essay topics

1 Discuss the importance of dance forms in the works of the English virginalists (Byrd, Bull, Gibbons, etc.).

2 Which were the 'new' dances of the seventeenth century, and how soon did they appear in the suite?

3 To what extent is the eighteenth century suite an international collection of dances?

4 Trace the origin of the French peasant dances that were brought to the court of Louis XIV.

5 In what way is the growth of the musical nationalism reflected in the choice of dance forms?

6 Describe the influence of the waltz in nineteenth century music.

7 Discuss the reasons for the general neglect of twentieth century dances by modern composers.

8 To what extent have modern composers taken an interest in the dances of earlier times?

9 Compare and contrast the characteristics of a suite of the mid-seventeenth century with one of the mid-eighteenth.

10 Which dances, in your opinion, have given the most inspiration to instrumental composers?

Index